Norman Tower, Bury St. Edmunds by A.Heaton Cooper

FA
SU
RECIPES

compiled by
Dorothy Baldock

SALMON

Index

Cover pictures: *front* Willy Lott's Cottage, Flatford by W.C. Affleck
back The Market Cross, Lavenham by A. Heaton Cooper

Printed and Published by J. Salmon Ltd., Sevenoaks, England ©

SUFFOLK RUSKS

8 oz. self-raising flour
Pinch of salt
3 oz. butter
1 egg, beaten
A little milk or water

Set oven to 450°F or Mark 8. Sift the flour and salt together into a bowl, then rub in the butter until the mixture resembles fine breadcrumbs. Stir in the beaten egg and sufficient milk or water to make a smooth dough. Roll out on a lightly floured surface to about 1 inch in thickness then cut into 2½ inch rounds. Place on a greased baking sheet and cook for 10 minutes. Remove from the oven and split in half. Reduce the oven temperature to 375°F or Mark 5. Return the Rusks to the baking sheet, cut side upwards, and cook for a further 10 to 15 minutes until crisp and golden-brown. Cool on a wire rack. Serve with butter and jam at teatime or as a savoury with cheese or Bloater Savoury. Suffolk Rusks store well in a tin.

A Mill on the River Gipping by A. R. Quinton

SUFFOLK RAISIN ROLY-POLY

3 oz. flour
Pinch of salt
1 teaspoon baking powder
4 oz. suet
12 oz. raisins, stoned
1 dessertspoon sugar

Mix the flour, salt and baking powder together, then add the suet and sufficient cold water to form a soft dough. Turn out on to a lightly floured surface and roll into an oblong about ¼ inch thick. Sprinkle the raisins and the sugar on to the dough, then roll up like a Swiss Roll, damping the ends and pressing firmly together to seal. Sprinkle with a little flour, then wrap lightly in greaseproof paper and roll up in a lightly floured pudding cloth, tying the ends tightly. Place in a saucepan of boiling water and boil for 3 hours, topping up the water as necessary. Serve cut into thick slices, and sprinkled with a little granulated sugar and accompanied by custard. Serves 4 to 6.

Baked Flounder

4 flounders
2 tablespoons finely chopped parsley
2 tablespoons finely chopped chives
2 tablespoons finely chopped tarragon
¼ teaspoon nutmeg
1 glass white wine
Salt and black pepper
2 oz. butter
4 oz. fresh white breadcrumbs
Parsley sprigs to garnish

If necessary, 4 small plaice can be substituted for the flounders.

Set oven to 450°F or Mark 8. Wash and dry the flounders. Mix the herbs and nutmeg together. Butter an ovenproof dish and coat with the herb mixture. Arrange the fish in the dish and pour the wine over. Season to taste. Melt 1 oz. of butter, pour on to the fish and cover with the breadcrumbs. Dot with the remaining butter and bake for 10 to 15 minutes, near the top of the oven, so that the breadcrumbs brown, adding a little extra butter if they look dry. Serve, garnished with parsley sprigs. Serves 2.

Pork with Prunes

8 oz. prunes, soaked, stoned
and chopped
(reserve the soaking liquid)
3 oz. fresh white breadcrumbs
1 to 2 tablespoons onions,
chopped finely
A little butter
2 fillets pork, trimmed and cut
in half crosswise
Salt and black pepper
3 oz. butter, melted
1½ oz. flour
¼ pint water or pork stock
¼ pint double cream
1 dessertspoon brandy

To make the sauce less rich,
replace the cream with milk.

Set oven to 350°F or Mark 4. Mix prunes and breadcrumbs together. Lightly fry onion in a little butter and mix with the prune mixture. Cut each pork fillet in half lengthwise and spread lower halves with the prune mixture. Cover with the top halves and tie with string. Dust fillets with seasoned flour, adding extra seasoning if desired. Place in an ovenproof dish, pour melted butter over, cover and cook for 40 minutes. Remove from oven and pour off liquid into a pan. Return fillets to oven and cook, uncovered, for further 15 to 20 minutes to brown. Blend the flour into the liquid, then add reserved prune liquid and water or stock. Bring to boil, stirring; boil for 3 minutes. Stir in cream and brandy and heat through; do not boil. Remove strings from fillets, place on a dish and pour the sauce over. Serves 2.

SUFFOLK TRIFLE

4 large macaroons
4 tablespoons white wine
1 tablespoon brandy
½ pint single cream
1 egg and 1 egg yolk
½ to 1 tablespoon cornflour
½ oz. caster sugar
2 to 3 oz. raspberry jam
1 oz. blanched almonds
1 oz. candied peel, chopped
½ pint double cream

Put the macaroons in a glass bowl and pour over the wine and brandy. Leave macaroons to soak, adding extra wine or brandy if they appear dry. Pour the single cream into a pan and warm gently until just on the point of boiling. Beat together the egg, egg yolk and cornflour in a bowl, pour on the cream and whisk lightly. Return to a clean saucepan and cook gently, without boiling, until custard has thickened, stirring continuously. Stir in the sugar and allow the custard to cool a little. Pour over the soaked macaroons and set in a cool place. Carefully smooth the jam over the custard, then sprinkle with almonds and candied peel. Whip the double cream until it stands in soft peaks and pipe or pile on top of trifle. Serve decorated with extra blanched almonds and candied peel, if desired. Serves 4.

The Old Moot Hall, Sudbury by A. Heaton Cooper

Bloater Savoury

2 bloaters
2 oz. butter, softened
2 teaspoons Worcestershire sauce
Cayenne pepper to taste
2 egg yolks
A squeeze of lemon juice

Grill the bloaters on both sides, then remove the skin and bones and flake the flesh. Add the butter to the fish and blend well. Stir in the Worcestershire sauce and cayenne pepper. Bind with the egg yolks and lemon juice. Sieve to produce a smooth paste and turn into a dish. Serve with fingers of hot toast or Suffolk Rusks.

This hot spicy paste was very popular in Edwardian times, when it was served with toast or Suffolk Rusks as an appetizer or a savoury. If bloaters are not available, it can be made with smoked mackerel.

Mushroom Pudding

8 oz. self-raising flour
Pinch of salt
3 oz. suet
1 small onion, peeled and sliced
1 lb. mushrooms, wiped, trimmed and sliced
4 rashers streaky bacon, chopped
Salt and black pepper
A little water or stock

Mix the flour, salt and suet together then add sufficient cold water to form a soft dough. Turn out onto a lightly floured surface and roll out. Use ⅔ of the dough to line a greased 2 pint pudding basin, reserving the remaining ⅓ for the lid. Seal any gaps well. Mix the onion, mushrooms and bacon together, season, and put into the centre of the pudding, adding a little stock or water. Add the dough lid, pressing the edges firmly together and sealing with a little water. Tie a circle of greaseproof paper over the basin and cover securely with kitchen foil. Place on a stand in a saucepan, and pour round sufficient boiling water to come about half way up the basin. Cover and boil for 2 to 2½ hours, topping up with boiling water as necessary. Serve with potatoes and a green vegetable. Serves 4.

CRAG PATH & BEACH, ALDEBURGH.

Crag Path and the Beach, Aldeburgh by C. T. Howard

SUFFOLK FISH PIE

2 lb. cod or haddock fillets
1 pint milk
Salt and black pepper
3 hard-boiled eggs, shelled
2 oz. butter
2 oz. flour
2 tablespoons chopped parsley
1 teaspoon chopped capers
1 lb. mashed potatoes

Set oven to 375°F or Mark 5. Cook the fish in the milk in a saucepan, seasoning to taste. Reserve the milk and flake the fish. Butter a deep 2 to 2½ pint pie dish and put the fish into it. Slice the hard-boiled eggs and lay on top of the fish. Melt the butter and stir in the flour, then add the reserved milk and cook, stirring, until thickened. Stir in the parsley and capers, and season to taste. Pour this sauce over the fish and eggs. Cover with mashed potato, 'roughing' it up lightly with a fork. Dot with a little butter and cook for 30 minutes or until the potato is lightly browned. Serve with a green vegetable, such as buttered spinach. Serves 4. If desired, a layer of sliced tomato can be placed on top of the fish, before the potato topping is added.

GOOSEBERRY CUSTARD

2 lb. gooseberries, topped and tailed
½ pint water
1 oz. butter
1 tablespoon rosewater or lemon juice
6 to 8 oz. sugar
½ pint double cream
4 eggs

Wash the gooseberries and drain well. Put in a saucepan with the water and simmer until soft. Mash gently with a fork, then stir in the butter, rosewater or lemon juice and sugar and cook gently until the sugar is completely dissolved. Whisk the cream and eggs together, then stir into the gooseberry mixture. Cook over a low heat, stirring, until thickened. Pour into a serving bowl and chill. Serve with boudoir or cat's tongue biscuits. Serves 4 to 6.

This very old recipe is a forerunner of the more modern Gooseberry Fool. 'Custard' was the usual Suffolk description of a creamy dessert or pudding.

SUFFOLK 'FOURSES' CAKE

1½ lb. strong flour
½ teaspoon salt
2 teaspoons mixed spice
½ oz. yeast
2 teaspoons sugar
¾ pint warm water
6 oz. lard
6 oz. currants

This currant bread was eaten by farm-workers in the fields at teatime.

Sift the flour, salt and spice together. Cream the yeast and sugar together with a little of the water and allow to sponge. Rub the lard into the flour, make a well in the centre and add the yeast mixture. Stir in the remaining water to form a smooth dough. Turn out on to a lightly floured surface and knead thoroughly. Cover and leave to rise in a warm place until the dough has doubled in bulk. Knead again, adding the currants so that they are well distributed in the dough. Divide the dough into two lightly greased 1 lb. loaf tins. Cover and leave to prove in a warm place. Set oven to 400°F or Mark 6; when the dough has risen to about 1 inch above the top of the tins bake for 45 minutes. While still warm brush the tops of the loaves with a little water or milk to give a slight sheen. Serve plain or spread with butter.

IPSWICH ALMOND PUDDING

¾ pint milk
5 fluid oz. double cream
2 oz. fresh white breadcrumbs, finely grated
3 oz. sugar
6 oz. ground almonds
1 teaspoon orange flower water or rose water
3 eggs, beaten
1 oz. butter

Set oven to 350°F or Mark 4. Warm the milk and cream together in a saucepan; put the breadcrumbs in a bowl, then add the milk/cream mixture and leave to stand for 5 minutes. Add the sugar, ground almonds and orange water or rose water and leave to stand for a further 10 minutes until all the liquid has been absorbed. Stir in the eggs, blending well. Pour the mixture into a buttered 2 pint pie dish. Dot the surface with the butter. Set the pie dish in a roasting tin. Pour boiling water into the tin until it comes about a quarter of the way up the side of the pie dish. Bake for 30 minutes. Serve accompanied by single cream. Serves 4.

THE ANCIENT HOUSE, IPSWICH.

The Ancient House, Ipswich by A. R. Quinton

Duck and Green Peas

1 oven-ready duck, about
4–6 lb in weight
Salt and black pepper
16 to 20 baby onions, peeled
2 oz. streaky bacon rashers, diced
1 lb. peas, fresh or frozen
4 tablespoons chicken stock
Sprigs of fresh herbs: parsley,
mint, thyme

Allow about 30 minutes for each
pound in weight of the duck.

Set oven to 350°F or Mark 4. Prick the duck skin with a fork and rub with salt and pepper; place on a wire rack in a roasting tin and cook. About 30 minutes before the end of the cooking time, drain off the fat in the roasting tin and keep the duck warm whilst preparing the vegetables. Place 2 to 3 tablespoons of the fat in a saucepan, cook the onions until lightly browned, then add the bacon and cook for a further 2 minutes. Cook the peas, if fresh, in boiling water for 2 to 3 minutes and drain well. (Do not cook the peas if frozen.) Add the peas to the onion mixture, with the stock and the herbs and season to taste. Pour into the roasting tin, stirring lightly, replace the duck, still on the wire rack and continue cooking. Serve the duck surrounded by the vegetables mixture and accompanied by creamed potatoes. Serves 4.

SUFFOLK DUMPLINGS

8 oz. flour
Pinch of salt
½ pint cold water

Mix the flour and salt together, then add the water, mixing to form a firm dough. Roll into 6 to 8 balls with floured hands, then roll in a little extra flour. Put into a saucepan of fast boiling water, cover and boil hard for 20 minutes. Drain well and serve immediately with rich, brown gravy as a starter or part of a main course or with melted butter or golden syrup as a dessert. Serves 3 or 4. If the dumplings are intended as a dessert, a few currants can be added to the dough before boiling.

Suffolk Dumplings, also known as Hard Dumplings, should be eaten with two forks, being pulled apart to let out the steam.

Walberswick Ferry by A. Heaton Cooper

POTTED SHRIMPS

1 lb. shelled shrimps
1 teaspoon mace
8 oz. butter
Pinch of cayenne pepper

Chop half the shrimps finely then mix with the remaining whole shrimps and stir in the mace. Melt 6 oz. butter in a saucepan, add the shrimps, stirring until they have absorbed all the butter. Stir in the cayenne pepper. Turn the mixture into ramekins, pressing down well. Melt the remaining 2 oz. butter and pour over the shrimp mixture to seal. Allow to cool and place in the refrigerator for several hours or preferably overnight. Serve with hot toast, cut into fingers. Serves 4 to 6.

GREENGAGE TART

8 oz. shortcrust pastry
1 lb. greengages, washed, halved and stoned
1 dessertspoon sugar, optional
2 eggs, beaten
1 pint single cream

Set oven to 400°F or Mark 6. Line a 7 inch flan dish with the pastry and bake blind for 10 minutes. Arrange the greengages, cut side down, in the pastry case, and sprinkle with the sugar, if desired. Beat the eggs and cream together, and strain over the greengages. Cook for 30 to 35 minutes or until the filling is golden and puffed up. Serve warm with extra cream, if desired. Serves 4.

In the 18th century, Sir William Gage planted some unknown plum trees in the orchard of his estate near Bury Saint Edmunds. They produced delicious yellow-green fruit, that became known as Green Gage's Plums, later corrupted to Greengage.

SPINACH SOUP

2 lb. spinach, washed and shredded
1 small turnip, peeled and finely chopped
2 carrots, peeled and finely chopped
2 small onions, peeled and finely chopped
1 stick celery, washed, trimmed and finely chopped
1 tablespoon chopped parsley
1 teaspoon chopped thyme
2 oz. uncooked rice
2½ to 3 pints chicken stock
1 oz. butter
Salt and black pepper

At one time spinach soup would also include a few young nettles in its ingredients.

Place the vegetables, herbs and rice in a saucepan and pour 1 pint of the stock over. Bring to the boil, stirring, then cover and simmer for 30 minutes, stirring regularly. Allow to cool a little, then mash or liquidize the mixture. Return the mixture to a clean saucepan, add the remainder of the stock, the butter and seasoning. Bring to the boil and boil for 3 to 4 minutes, stirring. Serve garnished, if desired, with a few croutons. Serves 4 to 6.

The traditional accompaniment to this soup is a few tiny suet dumplings, cooked in advance and dropped into the soup immediately before serving.

SUFFOLK HARVEST CAKE

8 oz. flour
2 oz. cornflour
1 teaspoon baking powder
¼ teaspoon bicarbonate of soda
¼ teaspoon ground nutmeg
¼ teaspoon ground cinnamon
½ oz. fresh yeast, finely crumbled
8 oz. sugar
4 oz. lard or butter
¼ pint milk
1 egg
½ lb. currants or sultanas
2 oz. chopped candied lemon
or orange peel

Set oven to 350°F or Mark 4. Sift together the flour, cornflour, baking powder, bicarbonate of soda and spices. Rub in the crumbled yeast, then stir in the sugar. Cut the fat into flakes and rub into the dry ingredients. Beat together the milk and egg and stir into the mixture; then add the dried fruit and candied peel and combine well together. Turn into a well-greased and lined 10 inch cake tin. Cover and leave in a warm place for 30 minutes to rise; then cook for 2 hours, covering the top of the cake if it browns too quickly. When removed from the oven the top of the cake can be lightly brushed with a little milk, while still hot, to give a sheen. Serve in slices, either plain or spread with butter.

KERSEY, SUFFOLK

A.R.QUINTON

Kersey from the church by A.R. Quinton

Rabbit Pie

12 oz. shortcrust pastry
8 rabbit joints
8 oz. belly pork, cubed
2 onions, peeled and chopped
2 sprigs parsley, 1 sprig thyme,
3 sage leaves and 1 bayleaf
tied together with string
½–¼ pint water or chicken stock
Salt and black pepper

Put the rabbit joints, belly pork, onion, herbs and water or stock into a casserole and season to taste. Cover and cook for 1 to 1½ hours or until the rabbit joints are tender, topping up with water or stock as necessary. Discard the herbs and turn the stew into a large deep pie dish. Allow to cool. Set oven to 325°F or Mark 3. Roll out the pastry on a lightly floured surface to form an oval. Damp the edges of the pie dish and put on the pastry lid, trimming the edges neatly. Use the trimmings for decoration. Brush the pastry with a little milk or beaten egg to glaze. Increase the oven temperature to 400°F or Mark 6 and cook the pie for 40 to 50 minutes, or until the top is golden brown. Serve with potatoes and swedes mashed together with butter and milk, carrots and a green vegetable. Serves 4 to 6.

BROTHERLY LOVE

1 lb. flour
1 teaspoon salt
2 oz. lard
½ oz. yeast
1 dessertspoon caster sugar
½ pint warm water
2 oz. granulated sugar

The Suffolk version of the popular lardy cake.

Set oven to 425°F or Mark 7. Mix the flour and salt together, then rub in 1 oz. of the lard. Cream the yeast with the sugar and stir in the water and allow to sponge. Make a well in the flour and add the yeast mixture. Mix well then turn out on to a lightly floured surface. Knead, then cover and leave in a warm place until the dough has doubled in bulk. Knead again, then roll out into an oblong ½ inch thick. Flake the remaining lard and dot evenly over the dough, then sprinkle the sugar over. Roll up like a Swiss Roll, put on to a greased baking sheet and bake for 30 minutes. When removed from the oven brush the top with a little milk while warm to give a sheen. An alternative way of baking Brotherly Love is to cut the 'Swiss Roll' into 1 inch slices and put on a greased baking sheet to cook for 30 minutes.

The Pier Head, Lowestoft by A. R. Quinton

Lowestoft Herrings

8 herrings, cleaned
2 to 3 pints salt water: use fresh
water salted to a rate of 2 oz. salt
to 1 pint of water

MUSTARD SAUCE
1 oz. butter
1 level tablespoon flour
1 well-rounded teaspoon dry mustard
Pinch of salt
Squeeze of lemon juice
½ pint fish stock
1 tablespoon white wine vinegar

Place the herrings in the salted water, which has been brought to a rolling boil. Bring back to the boil and boil quickly for 8 to 10 minutes. Drain well, and serve with boiled potatoes and Mustard Sauce. Serves 4.

Mustard Sauce: melt the butter over a low heat and add the flour, stirring until the mixture is smooth. Remove from the heat and add the mustard, salt and lemon juice. Gradually stir in the stock and the vinegar. Bring to the boil, stirring, and pour over the Lowestoft Herrings to serve.

Originally these herrings were boiled in fresh sea water, as this was considered to make the flesh appetizingly firm.

STONE CREAM

5 oz. apricot or strawberry jam
1 teaspoon lemon juice
1 pint double cream
1 oz. caster sugar
½ oz. gelatine
2 tablespoons water
Extra cream to decorate

If preferred, fresh apricots that have been lightly poached or fresh strawberries can be substituted for jam.

Mix the jam and the lemon juices together and spread over the base of a glass serving bowl. Pour the cream into a thick-bottomed saucepan, stir in the sugar and heat gently until the sugar has dissolved and the cream is warm. Dissolve the gelatine in the water, stir gently into the cream and pour over the jam. Leave in a cool place until set, then whip the extra cream and decorate with piped rosettes or stars. Serves 4.

Oxtail Brawn

1 oxtail, washed, dried and
cut into joints
1 oz. butter
1 onion, peeled, left whole and
stuck with 6 cloves
3 sprigs parsley, 1 sprig thyme,
1 small sage leaf and 1 small bayleaf,
tied together with string
Salt and black pepper
2 tablespoons vinegar
1 egg

This is a delicious Suffolk alternative to
the more usual pig's head brawn.

Dust the jointed oxtail with seasoned flour. Melt the butter in a saucepan and fry the oxtail until lightly browned on all sides. Add the onion, herbs, seasoning and vinegar, then add sufficient cold water to cover. Bring to the boil, cover, and simmer for about 4 hours, until the meat leaves the bones. Cool, then chop the meat, reserving both the bones and the liquid, but discarding the herbs and onion. Butter a pudding basin. Hard-boil the egg, shell and slice; arrange the slices decoratively in the base of the basin. Add the meat. Boil the bones until the liquid has been reduced to about ½ pint. Cool slightly, then strain into the basin. Cover with a plate or saucer and put in the refrigerator to set. Turn out when completely cold and set and serve sliced, with salad or boiled potatoes and green peas.

Suffolk Cakes

2 oz. butter
2 eggs
4 oz. caster sugar
Finely grated rind of a small lemon
2 oz. self-raising flour

Set oven to 400°F or Mark 6. Warm the butter in a saucepan until it is *just* liquid. Separate the eggs and whisk the whites until they stand in soft peaks. Beat the yolks, add the sugar and lemon rind, then fold in the egg whites. Stir the butter and flour into the egg mixture and beat well. Divide the mixture evenly between paper bun cases that have been set in a bun tin (the mixture is somewhat 'slack' so placing the paper cases in a bun tin gives them extra support) and bake for about 15 minutes or until the cakes are golden and springy to the touch. As the cakes cool, their tops will flatten.

Long Melford by A. Heaton Cooper

Onion Pudding

4 oz. flour
2 oz. shredded suet
½ lb. onions, peeled and
finely chopped
Salt and black pepper

Mix the flour and suet together then add sufficient cold water to form a firm dough. Turn out on to a lightly floured surface and roll out to form a oblong about about ¼ inch thick. Sprinkle the onion over the dough, and season well. Roll up like a Swiss Roll and damp the ends to seal. Wrap lightly in greaseproof paper, then tie up in a cloth. Place in a saucepan of boiling water, cover and cook for 1 to 1½ hours; alternatively steam similarly. Top up with boiling water as necessary. Serve cut into thick slices, each slice topped with a pat of butter, as an accompaniment to boiled bacon or boiled beef. Serves 4.

A cottager's pudding, often served with a piece of boiled bacon and, by tradition, cooked in the same pot.

IPSWICH LEMON PIE

8 oz. shortcrust pastry
Grated rind and juice of a lemon
2 oz. butter
4 oz. caster sugar
4 eggs, beaten

Set oven to 400°F or Mark 6. Line a 7 inch flan dish with the pastry. Put the lemon rind and juice, butter and sugar into a saucepan and heat gently until the sugar has completely dissolved, stirring as little as possible. Allow the mixture to cool completely, then strain the beaten eggs into it and stir gently until combined. Pour the mixture into the pastry case, and brush the edges of the pie with milk to glaze. Cook for 10 minutes, then reduce the oven temperature to 350°F or Mark 4 for a further 15 to 20 minutes, until the filling is set and the pastry lightly golden. Serve hot or cold with cream. Serves 4.

SOUTHWOLD, GUN HILL

AR QUINTON

Gun Hill, Southwold by A. R. Quinton

SHRIMPS AND LETTUCE IN CREAM

1 lb. prepared shrimps, fresh or frozen
2 large cos lettuce hearts, washed, drained and finely shredded
2 oz. butter, melted
¼ pint double cream
1 teaspoon onion juice, made by crushing a small, peeled onion or alternatively a little *very* finely chopped onion
Salt and black pepper
4 slices of bread
A little butter for frying

Thaw the shrimps if frozen and reserve a few for garnish. Place the lettuce and melted butter in a saucepan, and turn the lettuce with a wooden spoon until it is completely coated with the butter, then cover and simmer *very* gently for 3 to 4 minutes, stirring occasionally. Stir in the cream and the onion juice or chopped onion and season to taste. Stir in the shrimps and heat through for 2 to 3 minutes, but *do not* allow to boil. Set aside and keep warm. Cut the bread into neat triangles and fry lightly in butter. Keep warm. Pile the shrimp mixture on to a dish and arrange the bread triangles around the edge. Serve, garnished with the reserved shrimps. Serves 4 to 6.

A summer dinner party dish that comes from the Southwold area.

Pickled Eggs

8 eggs
1 pint white vinegar
¼ oz. black peppercorns
¼ oz. allspice berries
¼ oz. root ginger, lightly bruised

Boil the eggs for 10 minutes. Cool in cold water, then shell. In a saucepan simmer the vinegar and spices together for 5 minutes. Place the eggs in a warmed sterilized jar and pour the hot vinegar mixture over, leaving in the spices. Cover and store in a cool dry place for about 2 weeks to allow the pickled eggs to mature. Serve with cold meats or cold poultry or game.

Ham Toasts

2 tablespoons double cream
8 oz. ham, finely chopped
4 slices of bread, toasted, buttered
and kept warm
1 oz. butter
2 tablespoons milk
8 eggs
Salt and black pepper
Parsley sprigs to garnish

Put the cream and ham in a saucepan and heat thoroughly. Spread on to the toast and keep warm. Melt the butter in a saucepan. Beat the milk and eggs together, seasoning to taste, and add to the melted butter, stirring until the egg mixture is lightly scrambled. Pile on to the ham mixture, and serve at once, garnished with parsley sprigs. Serves 4.

Pork and Red Cabbage

1 lb. red cabbage, washed and shredded
1 large cooking apple, peeled, cored and sliced
1 tablespoon brown sugar
2 tablespoons cider vinegar
1 tablespoon flour
Salt and black pepper
1½ lb. boneless pork shoulder, the rind removed
Parsley sprigs to garnish

Set oven to 375°F or Mark 5. Bring a large saucepan of water, to which 1 tablespoon of cider vinegar has been added, to the boil. Add the cabbage and bring back to the boil, then drain the cabbage very well. Place the cabbage and the apple in a casserole, then stir in the sugar, the remaining cider vinegar, the flour and seasoning. Slash the fat side of the pork shoulder and rub in a little salt and pepper, then place on top of the cabbage mixture. Cover and cook for about 1½ to 2 hours or until the pork is tender. Slice the pork and arrange the slices on a warmed serving dish, surrounded by the cabbage mixture. Garnish with parsley and serve with creamed potatoes. Serves 4.

Beccles from the River Waveney by A. Heaton Cooper

BLACKBERRY SYRUP

1 lb. blackberries
½ pint white wine vinegar
½ lb. sugar
4 oz. honey

Place the blackberries in a glass or china bowl and pour the vinegar over. Leave to stand for at least 24 hours, stirring and pressing the fruit regularly, to extract the juices. Strain the liquid into a large saucepan or small preserving pan and bring to the boil. Add the sugar, stirring until it is all dissolved, then add the honey, stirring well. Bring back to the boil and boil hard for 5 minutes. Allow to cool completely. Originally this syrup was bottled and stored, one tablespoon being added to a glass of hot water to form a bedtime drink. However, the syrup can easily be frozen in ice-cube trays and then stored in bags in the freezer to be used when required.

A pleasant nightcap that is also said to be good for relieving a cold.

SUFFOLK TROUT

4 trout, cleaned
4 bayleaves
2 oz. butter
Juice of a lemon
Salt and black pepper
Lemon slices to garnish

Remove the heads from the trout and slip a bayleaf inside each fish. Melt the butter in a large, thick-bottomed frying pan, put in the trout and pour the lemon juice over. Season lightly. Cover the pan and cook the trout over a *very* low heat for 20 minutes, turning once. Serve, garnished with lemon slices, and accompanied by boiled potatoes and peas. Serves 4.

Monks Eleigh by A. R. Quinton

Suffolk Buns

12 oz. flour
4 oz. ground rice
2 teaspoons baking powder
4 oz. butter
3 oz. sugar
1½ oz. caraway seeds
2 eggs, beaten
Milk

Set oven to 400°F or Mark 6. Mix the flour, ground rice and baking powder together. Rub in the butter until the mixture resembles fine breadcrumbs, then stir into it the sugar and caraway seeds. Stir in the eggs, and sufficient milk to make a smooth firm paste. Turn out on to a lightly floured surface and roll out to 1 inch in thickness. Cut into 2 inch rounds and place on a greased baking sheet. Bake for 15 to 20 minutes until golden.

If desired, 3 oz. currants can be substituted for the caraway seeds, though the caraway seeds are a more traditional ingredient.

Vegetable Pie

POTATO PASTRY
6 oz. margarine
8 oz. self-raising flour
Pinch of salt
8 oz. cold mashed potato
A little milk

VEGETABLE FILLING
8 oz. mixed vegetables; carrots, peas, celery etc.
A 'walnut' of butter
1 onion, peeled and chopped
4 oz. mushrooms, wiped and sliced
1 heaped teaspoon chopped parsley
¼ pint white sauce
Salt and black pepper
3 oz. Cheddar cheese, grated

Set oven to 400°F or Mark 6. Potato Pastry; rub margarine into the flour and salt until mixture resembles breadcrumbs. Combine with mashed potato, adding milk to produce a soft dough. Turn on a floured surface and knead lightly. Roll out and line a greased, large ovenproof dish. The pastry may be a little 'short' so handle carefully. Bake blind for 15 minutes, then cool a little. The Filling; chop and lightly cook the vegetables, drain well and cool a little. Melt butter and lightly fry onion and mushrooms. Combine with mixed vegetables, add parsley and stir in the white sauce, seasoning to taste. Put into the pastry case and level top. Sprinkle with grated cheese and brush pastry rim with milk. Bake for further 15 to 20 minutes, until pastry is golden and cheese melted and bubbling. Serves 4 to 6.

LOWESTOFT BUTTONS

4 oz. flour
6 fl oz. milk
Salt and black pepper
2 oz. butter
1 oz. fresh white breadcrumbs

Sieve the flour into a bowl and make a well in the centre. Gradually pour in the milk, stirring until a thick batter that will *just* drop from a spoon when shaken is formed. Season to taste. Drop teaspoons of the batter into a saucepan of fast-boiling water. Cover and boil for 5 minutes. Remove the 'buttons' with a slotted spoon, draining well, and pile on a hot serving dish. In a frying pan melt the butter and stir in the bread crumbs. Fry until golden, then sprinkle over the 'buttons'. Serve at once on their own or with a little melted butter poured over the buttons. Serves 4.

A popular light supper dish; also known as Spoon Dumplings.

METRIC CONVERSIONS

The weights, measures and oven temperatures used in the preceding recipes can be easily converted to their metric equivalents.

Weights

Avoirdupois	Metric
1 oz.	just under 30 grams
4 oz. (¼ lb.)	app. 115 grams
8 oz. (½ lb.)	app. 230 grams
1 lb.	454 grams

Liquid Measures

Imperial	Metric
1 tablespoon (liquid only)	20 millilitres
1 fl. oz.	app. 30 millilitres
1 gill (¼ pt.)	app. 145 millilitres
½ pt.	app. 285 millilitres
1 pt.	app. 570 millilitres
1 qt.	app. 1.140 litres

Oven Temperatures

	°Fahrenheit	Gas Mark	°Celsius
Slow	300	2	140
	325	3	158
Moderate	350	4	177
	375	5	190
	400	6	204
Hot	425	7	214
	450	8	232
	500	9	260

Flour as specified in these recipes refers to Plain Flour unless otherwise described